The Abortion CONTROVERSY

Robert Lerose

San Diego, CA

© 2025 ReferencePoint Press, Inc.
Printed in the United States

For more information, contact:
ReferencePoint Press, Inc.
PO Box 27779
San Diego, CA 92198
www.ReferencePointPress.com

ALL RIGHTS RESERVED.
No part of this work covered by the copyright hereon may be reproduced or used in any form or by any means—graphic, electronic, or mechanical, including photocopying, recording, taping, web distribution, or information storage retrieval systems—without the written permission of the publisher.

LIBRARY OF CONGRESS CATALOGING-IN-PUBLICATION DATA

Names: Lerose, Robert, author.
Title: The abortion controversy / by Robert Lerose.
Description: San Diego, CA : ReferencePoint Press, Inc., 2025. | Includes bibliographical references and index.
Identifiers: LCCN 2024013335 (print) | LCCN 2024013336 (ebook) | ISBN 9781678207724 (library binding) | ISBN 9781678207731 (ebook)
Subjects: LCSH: Pro-choice movement--United States--Juvenile literature. | Abortion--Political aspects--United States--Juvenile literature. | Abortion--Law and legislation--United States--Juvenile literature.
Classification: LCC HQ767.5.U5 L47 2025 (print) | LCC HQ767.5.U5 (ebook) | DDC 362.1988/800973--dc23/eng/20240430
LC record available at https://lccn.loc.gov/2024013335
LC ebook record available at https://lccn.loc.gov/2024013336

CONTENTS

Introduction   **4**
Life After the *Dobbs* Decision

Chapter One   **10**
The Road to *Dobbs*

Chapter Two   **19**
Women at Risk

Chapter Three   **28**
Medical Professionals Under Fire

Chapter Four   **37**
The Quest to End Abortion

Chapter Five   **46**
Efforts to Restore Abortion Rights

Source Notes	55
Organizations to Contact	59
For Further Research	60
Index	61
Picture Credits	64
About the Author	64

INTRODUCTION

Life After the *Dobbs* Decision

In June 2022, the US Supreme Court declared that there is no constitutional right to abortion. In a case called *Dobbs v. Jackson Women's Health Organization*, a majority of the justices rescinded the 1973 *Roe v. Wade* decision that had made abortion legal for almost half a century. The *Dobbs* ruling canceled that nationwide protection and left it up to each state to decide for itself whether abortion should or should not be legal and what restrictions, if any, should apply. Reaction to the decision was swift and passionate, with a full range of emotions—elation, frustration, joy, anger, and confusion—on public display. Americans marched in the streets to celebrate or despair, while lawmakers rushed to pass a flurry of bills to either restrict or safeguard abortion access.

Lawmakers Respond

In some states, preexisting laws that had been dormant under *Roe* were immediately reinstated. These so-called trigger laws—laws that took effect or were triggered by the *Dobbs* decision—came into force in states such as Mississippi, Arkansas, Oklahoma, Missouri, and South Dakota. These laws completely prohibit or severely restrict abortions. "Today, the overruling of *Roe* . . . permits Missouri to renew its proud pro-life traditions and restore basic legal protection for the most fundamental of human rights—the right to life,"[1] Missouri attorney general Eric Schmitt said shortly after the court's decision was announced.

Legislators in other states took full advantage of the new power that *Dobbs* granted, proposing and passing new, restrictive laws. On June 28, 2022, just four days after the *Dobbs* decision, a bill was introduced in the South Carolina Senate that would make it a crime for anyone to aid or abet women seeking abortions. In March 2023, Wyoming became the first state to outlaw the use of so-called abortion pills, which enable women to end pregnancies in the privacy of their own homes. Idaho passed a law making it a crime, punishable by up to five years in prison, to help a minor in any way—such as giving them money, finding a doctor, or arranging an appointment—so they can travel to another state for an abortion without parental consent.

> "Today, the overruling of *Roe* . . . permits Missouri to renew its proud pro-life traditions and restore basic legal protection for the most fundamental of human rights—the right to life."[1]
>
> —Eric Schmitt, attorney general of Missouri

On June 24, 2022, the US Supreme Court (shown in an official 2021 portrait) overturned the constitutional right to abortion. The Court's monumental five-to-four ruling gave states the ability to allow, restrict, or ban abortion.

> "American women are having their rights taken by five unelected justices on the extremist . . . court."[2]
>
> —Chuck Schumer, Senate majority leader

Not all lawmakers rushed to restrict abortion. In states that have long supported legal abortions, elected officials expressed alarm over the sudden rush to deny abortions to women who need or want them. "American women are having their rights taken by five unelected justices on the extremist . . . court,"[2] asserted US Senate majority leader Chuck Schumer. To counter these actions, several states have taken measures to protect a woman's right to obtain an abortion. A month after the *Dobbs* decision, Massachusetts passed a law ensuring that patients would be covered for abortion by insurance companies without any extra expense. "Massachusetts remains steadfast in its commitment to protect access to reproductive health care services, especially in the aftermath of the Supreme Court's decision overturning *Roe v. Wade*,"[3] Governor Charlie Baker said. States such as California, Connecticut, Minnesota, Nevada, and Vermont have also been at the forefront of expanding or strengthening abortion access—both for women and doctors. In New York, for example, a new law gave doctors legal protection to prescribe and send abortion pills to women living in states where such medications are prohibited.

Public Reaction

Ordinary citizens are also making their voices heard. People who both support and oppose legal abortion are taking part in public protests. In November 2022, the Supreme Court was again the site of protest. Three spectators interrupted that day's oral arguments—which had nothing to do with *Dobbs*—by denouncing the court's decision before they were arrested and removed.

On the one-year anniversary of the *Dobbs* decision, citizens on both sides took to the streets in cities nationwide to express their feelings. "I'm absolutely livid that people think that they can interfere with medical decisions between a woman and her doctor,"[4] said Lynn Rust, a protester at a Women's March rally in Washington, DC. In Chicago, pro-life and pro-choice protesters faced off against each other in the street by holding their own opposing rallies. "The elected officials in Illinois are trying to turn us into the abortion capital of the middle of the country,"[5] said lawyer Peter Breen.

Dobbs has also energized citizens to become more involved in the electoral process. They have sought to elect leaders and pass ballot measures that reflect their views on abortion. The impact of these efforts can be seen in the results of the 2023 election races. Generally, pro-choice forces fared better across the United States, even in conservative-leaning states. A ballot measure to protect reproductive rights passed in Ohio. Pro-choice lawmakers in Virginia gained control of both legislative chambers. In Kentucky, a proposed amendment to the state constitution that would have denied the right to abortion failed.

Women Who Need or Want an Abortion

Much of the reaction to the *Dobbs* ruling has been loud and forceful—on both sides. But abortion is normally a very personal and usually private experience. Now that the procedure has been restricted or banned in many states, women (or couples) who need or want abortions are speaking out as well. In pro-choice states, obtaining an abortion is relatively easy: patients make an appointment, show up for the procedure on the designated day and time, and go home the same day with aftercare instructions. But for individuals who live in a state that now bans or restricts abortion, that process is infinitely more complicated. Those who have time, money, and means can look for a health care provider in another state where the procedure is legal. Those who lack the resources to pay for out-of-state travel and a possible overnight stay might not be able to obtain the care they need or want.

Anna and Tony were living near San Antonio, Texas, in 2023 when Anna realized she was pregnant. They already had six children. Although the couple had always wanted a big family, they were struggling financially. At one point, the hot water heater in their house broke and they could not afford to fix it. They had to bathe their kids in cold water. "All I could think about [was] I need an abortion because there's no way I can deal with everything going on now," Anna recalled. Because of Texas's new abortion restrictions, the closest abortion provider was in the neighboring state of New Mexico—an eight-hour drive away. Anna and Tony did not have the money to pay for the trip and the procedure and still have enough to cover their regular daily expenses. They called off their plans for an abortion and got ready for the birth of their seventh child. "I'm scared right now,"[6] Anna told an interviewer in June 2023.

Deep Divisions

Although much has changed since the *Dobbs* ruling, American attitudes toward abortion have not. Polls have long shown that a majority of Americans favor legal abortion. This is still the

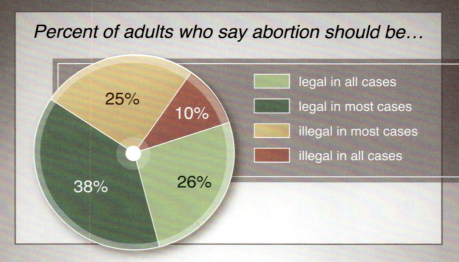

Strong Support for Legal Abortion

When asked for their views on whether abortion should be legal, 64 percent of poll respondents said they believe that abortion should be legal in all or most cases. This was the finding of a 2023 AP-NORC poll that sought to gauge public attitudes a year after *Roe v. Wade* was overturned by the US Supreme Court.

Percent of adults who say abortion should be...

- legal in all cases: 26%
- legal in most cases: 38%
- illegal in most cases: 25%
- illegal in all cases: 10%

Source: "Most Americans Support Legal Abortion with Some Restrictions," AP-NORC, July 12, 2023. www.apnorc.org.

case. When asked for their views on whether abortion should be legal, 64 percent of respondents in a 2023 AP-NORC poll said they believe that abortion should be legal in all or most cases. Despite the obstacles in many states, women are still seeking abortions. A report from the Guttmacher Institute found that in the year after *Dobbs*, the estimated number of abortions jumped 10 percent from 2020, the last year for which data was available. Far from settling the issue, the *Dobbs* decision has ushered in a contentious new phase.

CHAPTER ONE

The Road to *Dobbs*

In 1973, in a case called *Roe v. Wade*, the US Supreme Court ruled that the Constitution protects a woman's right to abortion. For the first time since the 1800s, women all across the country had the legal right to decide for themselves whether to end a pregnancy. Although there would be many attempts to weaken and even repeal the decision, *Roe* stood for nearly fifty years.

Public Shock

All that changed on June 24, 2022. On that date, the Supreme Court overturned the *Roe* ruling by a five-to-four vote. The court majority stated that the Constitution does not protect the right to obtain an abortion. The ruling in *Dobbs v. Jackson Women's Health Organization* did not ban abortion. Instead, it stated that it was up to each individual state to decide whether to restrict abortion—or not. It states, "It is time to heed the Constitution and return the issue of abortion to the people's elected representatives."[7]

> "It is time to heed the Constitution and return the issue of abortion to the people's elected representatives."[7]
>
> —Samuel Alito, associate justice of the US Supreme Court

Justice Samuel Alito, who wrote the majority opinion, argued that abortion is like other issues not expressly mentioned or protected by the Constitution. It is up to the voters and their elected representatives to decide how to treat abortion. "In some States," Alito wrote, "voters may believe that the abortion right should be even more extensive than the right that *Roe* and *Casey* [another abortion case] recognized. Voters in other States may wish to impose tight restrictions based on their belief that abortion destroys an 'unborn human being.'"[8]

Politicians responded to the *Dobbs* ruling swiftly and passionately:

- President Joe Biden said, "Now, with *Roe* gone, let's be very clear: The health and life of women in this nation are now at risk."[9]
- Nancy Pelosi, the Speaker of the House of Representatives at the time, referred to *Dobbs* as "this cruel ruling," calling it "outrageous and heart-wrenching."[10]
- Former vice president Mike Pence said, "By overturning *Roe v. Wade*, the Supreme Court of the United States has given the American people a new beginning for life, and I commend the justices in the majority for having the courage of their convictions."[11]
- Mitch McConnell, the Senate minority leader, said, "This is an historic victory for the Constitution and for the most vulnerable in our society."[12]

But the reactions of ordinary people, more than elected officials, most eloquently expressed both the frustration and the jubilation that the *Dobbs* decision created. Cities across the country erupted with competing rallies and demonstrations. Standing in the shadow of an 8-foot-tall (2 m) fence surrounding the Supreme Court—erected because of safety concerns after a draft opinion of the *Dobbs* decision had been prematurely leaked in May—protesters on both sides of the issue converged on the courthouse steps to voice their views. "This has been a fight 30 years in the making to overturn women and people's fundamental rights to make decisions about their

> "This is an historic victory for the Constitution and for the most vulnerable in our society."[12]
>
> —Mitch McConnell, Senate minority leader

Responding to news of the Supreme Court's Dobbs ruling, abortion rights supporters rally in Lansing, Michigan. Protests by abortion rights supporters and opponents erupted in cities across the nation once the ruling was made public.

body. There is no coming back from this. There is no response other than outrage and action,"[13] said Sara Kugler of Washington, DC. An unnamed protester who took the opposite view said, "For 50 years, one-third of my generation has been slaughtered due to the violence of abortion. Well, the survivors have risen up and we will not stand for the dismemberment, and poisoning, [and] subjugation of the most at-risk among us any longer."[14]

The *Dobbs* decision made an enormous impact on society, but it did not settle the question of abortion. Rather, *Dobbs* is the latest milestone in the tumultuous history of abortion in the United States.

Early Attitudes and Laws

Abortion has been part of American life practically since the founding of the republic. Laws and attitudes surrounding it, however, have shifted dramatically over time.

During the early nineteenth century, abortion was considered acceptable until a woman could feel the fetus move inside her, typically around sixteen to twenty weeks into pregnancy. This was known as quickening. Abortions done after quickening were considered a crime. A woman who sought an abortion after this point in her pregnancy could be charged with a misdemeanor.

By the early twentieth century, however, abortion laws had changed considerably. The long tradition of women helping other women—with deliveries as well as abortions—did not sit well with the male-dominated medical establishment. University-trained male doctors began to slander and denigrate midwives—including those with extensive experience—as being uneducated and unskilled. Similar to the effect of the unsavory comments, criminalizing abortion would reduce the influence of midwives. Both actions were aimed at helping male doctors retain their role as primary health care providers for entire families.

The Woman Behind Jane Roe

When Norma McCorvey died in 2017 at the age of sixty-nine, she left behind a puzzling legacy. Under the name Jane Roe, she was the plaintiff in the 1973 *Roe v. Wade* Supreme Court case that legalized abortion. She never aspired to be a national figure. But after living a low-key life in the decade after *Roe*, McCorvey began to speak out. She participated in abortion rights rallies, gave speeches, and worked as a counselor at a Dallas-based health clinic for women.

Then, in a dramatic turnabout, McCorvey disavowed her role in the pro-choice movement and stepped forward as an antiabortion crusader. In 2005 she testified before a congressional committee, urging the repeal of *Roe*. Some have suggested that her conversion to Christianity and Catholicism might explain her switch. Others say that both sides used her in the abortion debates for their own purposes. In her 1994 memoir, *I Am Roe*, McCorvey wrote, "I wasn't the wrong person to become Jane Roe. I wasn't the right person to become Jane Roe. I was just the person who became Jane Roe, of *Roe v. Wade*. And my life story, warts and all, was a little piece of history."

Quoted in Meilan Solly, "Who Was Norma McCorvey, the Woman Behind *Roe v. Wade*?," *Smithsonian Magazine*, June 24, 2022. www.smithsonianmag.com.

Despite these changes in the law, women still sought out abortions—often at great risk. It was not uncommon for abortion providers to perform the procedure under unsafe conditions. There was little to no follow-up care if the woman developed complications after the procedure.

Other women tried to terminate pregnancies on their own. Some threw themselves down staircases in hopes of dislodging the fetus. Others consumed poison, thinking it would kill the life growing inside them. Some women twisted open metal hangars and inserted the end into the womb, hoping to puncture the embryonic sac surrounding the fetus. Others endured the emotional distress, humiliation, and isolation of finding someone to perform an abortion at a time when the procedure was prohibited.

Sometimes these methods worked and resulted in the death of the fetus. But many women died or were permanently maimed as a consequence of these desperate efforts to end their pregnancies. The Guttmacher Institute found that in 1965 alone, nearly two hundred women had died from illegal abortions nationwide. Because this refers only to abortions that were officially reported, experts believe the actual number of abortion-related deaths was probably higher.

The 1960s ushered in a new era of activism. Along with the civil rights and antiwar movements, efforts to decriminalize abortion gained momentum. In 1967, Colorado became the first state to pass a law permitting abortion in cases of rape or incest or if the woman's physical or mental health were in jeopardy. Three years later, in 1970, New York became the first state to permit abortion on demand up to the twenty-fourth week of pregnancy.

The Legal Right to Abortion

As a few states began to loosen their restrictions, women became emboldened to seek greater freedom and control over their own bodies. Arguably, the most consequential development arising from this heightened activism emerged in the state of Texas. A twenty-one-year-old woman named Norma McCorvey wanted to

Norma McCorvey (known in court documents as Jane Roe) sued Texas over a law preventing her from getting an abortion. That case made its way to the US Supreme Court. The court's 1973 ruling in Roe v. Wade *made abortion legal nationwide.*

get an abortion in September 1969. At the time, Texas state law allowed abortions only if the mother's life was in jeopardy. McCorvey's life was not in jeopardy, but this was her third pregnancy. Media reports eventually disclosed that she had battled drug and alcohol issues, been abused by her former husband, and had little money. Using the pseudonym Jane Roe, McCorvey sued Henry Wade, the Dallas County district attorney, in 1970 for the right to an abortion.

Specifically, McCorvey's lawyers argued that the US Constitution guarantees a right to privacy, which in turn protects a woman's right to obtain an abortion. Letting Texas's abortion laws stand, the lawyers said, would deny the privacy rights of McCorvey and all women. When the district court upheld the law and refused to allow the abortion to proceed, McCorvey's lawyers appealed. The case, known as *Roe v. Wade*, eventually made its way to the US Supreme Court in December 1971. It was too late for McCorvey. Without access to abortion, in June 1970 she gave birth to a baby girl, whom she then gave up for adoption.

The situation at the Supreme Court presented an unexpected problem. Two of the justices had retired shortly before the case got under way, leaving McCorvey's lawyers to make their oral arguments in front of only seven justices. In a 4-to-3 decision, the

15

justices ruled that Texas's abortion laws were unconstitutional. The matter looked to be settled until one of the justices decided that the case should be heard in front of a full bench of nine justices. Almost a year later, in October 1972, oral arguments were heard again. On January 22, 1973, in a seven-to-two decision, the court ruled in favor of Jane Roe. In the majority opinion, Justice Harry A. Blackmun—who had asked for the retrial—argued that the US Constitution granted an individual the right to privacy—which extended to having an abortion—writing "that unduly restrictive state regulation of abortion is unconstitutional."[15]

The court based its ruling on the Constitution's Fourteenth Amendment. The amendment refers to due process and equal protection under the law. In plain language, it protects individuals from state laws that might infringe on their rights. It reads, in part, "nor shall any state deprive any person of life, liberty, or property, without due process of law; nor deny to any person within its ju-

The "Undue Burden" Test

In 1992, thirty years before *Roe* was rescinded, another Supreme Court case came close to undoing the right to an abortion. In *Planned Parenthood of Southeastern Pennsylvania v. Casey*, lawyers for the state sought to protect Pennsylvania's abortion regulations. These included a twenty-four-hour mandatory waiting period before the procedure could be performed, making minors obtain parental consent before getting an abortion, and making married women inform their husbands about scheduling an abortion.

Lawyers for Planned Parenthood argued that these provisions put women at risk and caused unnecessary delays in obtaining an abortion that had been guaranteed under *Roe*. In a five-to-four decision, the court upheld *Roe*, but it kept most of the Pennsylvania provisions in place. However, the court also introduced a new question about whether these provisions resulted in an "undue burden," or a "substantial obstacle in the path of a woman seeking an abortion before the fetus attains viability." The justices decided that none of the provisions in *Casey* placed an undue burden on women. From now on, though, this new standard of undue burden would be considered in abortion cases, until *Roe* was finally overturned.

Planned Parenthood of Southeastern Pennsylvania v. Casey. www.oyez.org.

risdiction the equal protection of the laws."[16] The court interpreted the language and the intent of the amendment to cover unnamed rights, such as privacy. By this reasoning, the court decided that abortion fell under a woman's right to privacy, to be able to make decisions about her own body.

Although the *Roe* decision enshrined the legal right to abortion across the country, it did not allow for unrestricted abortions. Instead, the Supreme Court stated that the state had a "compelling interest"[17] in weighing the rights of both the pregnant woman and the fetus. In practical terms, abortion would be permitted without restriction until the end of the first trimester of pregnancy, or roughly twelve weeks. After that, the court decided, the state had the right to regulate abortion. It based its reasoning on the concept of viability, the point at which a fetus could exist independent of its mother.

The End of *Roe*

From the day *Roe* was decided, parties on both sides of the debate engaged in intense, heated, and sometimes violent disagreement. Public reaction revealed a gaping divide. Some Americans rejoiced in the knowledge that no woman in America would ever need to subject herself to the danger of an illegal abortion. Others opposed the ruling, which they equated to the killing of innocent life. Over the years, both sides mobilized to fight for their respective positions—raising money and electing like-minded people to office. Abortion opponents also filed lawsuits seeking to undermine or reverse *Roe*. Despite these legal challenges, *Roe* remained in force until June 2022.

The justices who ruled in favor of *Dobbs* disagreed with the logic of the *Roe* decision. First, they pointed out that the Constitution does not confer an explicit right to abortion. Second, they argued that the Fourteenth Amendment says nothing about the right to privacy. Third, they criticized viability—the point at which a fetus can live independently of its mother—as discretionary, inaccurate, and unsound. As Justice Samuel Alito, author of the

Dobbs opinion, wrote, "This arbitrary line has not found much support among philosophers and ethicists who have attempted to justify a right to abortion." Alito noted that medical advances over time have changed the point at which a fetus can be viable outside the womb. The viability line, he continued, "makes no sense, and it is telling that other countries almost uniformly eschew such a line."[18] Associate justices Clarence Thomas, Neil Gorsuch, Brett Kavanaugh, and Amy Coney Barrett concurred with Alito's reasoning. Chief justice John Roberts disagreed. He urged the court to not overturn *Roe*.

Their fellow justices—Stephen Breyer, Sonia Sotomayor, and Elena Kagan—opposed the majority ruling, issuing a joint dissenting opinion. Under *Dobbs*, they argued, a woman essentially loses her rights the moment a child is conceived. "Across a vast array of circumstances, a State will be able to impose its moral choice on a woman and coerce her to give birth to a child," the justices wrote in their dissent. "Under those laws, a woman will have to bear her rapist's child or a young girl her father's—no matter if doing so will destroy her life." The dissenting justices concluded that no matter what differences individual states might have in regulating abortion, "one result of today's decision is certain: the curtailment of women's rights, and of their status, as free and equal citizens."[19]

Despite the *Dobbs* decision, support for legal abortion remains high. In April 2023, almost a full year after the right to abortion had been declared unconstitutional, 61 percent of US adults in a *PBS NewsHour*/NPR/Marist poll said they favored protecting abortion freedoms. Antiabortion groups are undeterred by this countervailing public opinion. They see the *Dobbs* decision as bringing them one step closer to realizing their dream of banning abortion across the country under any circumstances. Undoing *Roe* took almost half a century. Both the pro-life and the pro-choice movements suffered setbacks and successes. No one can say with certainty what will come next in the nation's long abortion saga, but one thing is clear: the questions, issues, and conflicts in this debate will continue to vex US society for years to come.

CHAPTER TWO

Women at Risk

The *Dobbs* decision gave states the right to regulate abortion. State legislatures are now free to enact new laws. Conservative lawmakers who had passionately disagreed with *Roe* quickly passed new prohibitions on abortions. States with liberal majorities shored up protections for women and health care providers who perform abortions. The result has been a confusing patchwork of laws where neighboring states could have vastly different regulations. States such as California and Vermont added or expanded abortion freedoms to their constitutions. Kansas and Michigan protected or reaffirmed their existing abortion rights. South Carolina began enforcing a six-week ban on abortions, and Idaho enacted a near total ban on abortion procedures. Alabama banned abortion completely.

Hitting the Road

From the day the *Dobbs* ruling went into effect, the consequences have rippled out across the country. For some, those consequences have been devastating. Trying to make sense of a given state's laws and, at the same time, have access to essential reproductive medical services has put new pressure on women, their families, and their health care providers—a problem that did not exist when *Roe* was in effect. Thirty-one-year-old Jennifer Adkins of Idaho has experienced this pressure firsthand. At her twelve-week ultrasound appointment, Adkins and her husband, John, learned that their fetus had a rare condition in which an X chromosome was missing. Adkins's doctor told her that the chances of the fetus surviving until birth were essentially nil and that bringing the fetus to term could threaten Adkins's own life. But because of Idaho's severe abortion restrictions, Adkins's doctor could not perform the procedure. After an intense few days looking for a clinic and making arrangements, Adkins and her husband flew to Oregon for the procedure. "We felt like we were criminals,"[20] John Adkins said.

Under the best of circumstances, abortion can be a trying, serious, and emotional experience. For pregnant women who live in states where abortion is illegal or severely restricted, the pressure is substantially greater. Because they cannot use a local health care provider, they are forced to search for facilities in another state. Since *Dobbs*, there has been a surge in the number

Source: Kimya Forouzan et al., "The High Toll of US Abortion Bans: Nearly One in Five Patients Now Traveling Out of State for Abortion Care," Guttmacher Institute, December 7, 2023. www.guttmacher.org.

of women looking for out-of-state facilities. The result has been longer wait times to get an appointment or women being turned down completely because the facility simply cannot handle the crushing demand.

Assuming that an appointment can be booked, these women must then make long-distance travel arrangements and take time off from work—something that could be avoided if they could use a local health care provider. If they have other children, arrangements need to be made for someone to look after them. Since *Dobbs*, many women have had to travel far from home for an abortion. According to the Guttmacher Institute, 92,100 women went out of state for abortion care in the first half of 2023—more than double the number of women during the first half of 2020. This can mean long, uncomfortable road trips by car or bus—to the clinic and back home again. Beyond the costs associated with the procedure itself, women must also shoulder the added expenses for food, travel, and lodging.

Ashley Brandt of Texas knows the anguish of an out-of-state abortion experience. While pregnant, she learned that one of the twins she was carrying had acrania, a fatal condition. Under Texas law, doctors were prevented from performing an abortion or from taking any action until Brandt's condition worsened. "I would have had to give birth to an identical version of my daughter without a skull and without a brain and hold her until she died,"[21] Brandt testified in court. Brandt and a few other women have sued the state of Texas over provisions in its abortion law. They claim that they were denied medically necessary care because of the law's confusing language.

Rather than endure the wrenching experience of seeing one twin die in her arms, Brandt made the decision to get an abortion in Colorado—three states away from her Texas home. She found a facility and was able to arrange an appointment, but the episode left its mark on her. "It angers me that I had to travel out of state for a procedure that could have been done in a day here in my own community," Brandt says. "How can you call yourself 'pro-life' and support laws that force women to gamble with not only their own lives but their babies' lives? I don't understand the logic."[22]

The Cost of Denying Care

Jaci Statton of Oklahoma was about nine weeks pregnant when she was told by her doctor that her pregnancy was not viable. The doctor also informed her that, without an abortion, Statton risked terrible internal bleeding, the development of cancer tissue, or possibly death. Statton had no choice. She had three children at home to care for and could not gamble on losing her life in a pregnancy where the fetus would not survive anyhow. She decided that an abortion was the right, medically necessary action to take. What happened next turned into a personal nightmare. Statton's home state of Oklahoma outlaws most abortions. Because a fetal heartbeat had been detected during an ultrasound, the doctor could not legally perform an abortion. Statton was denied the procedure.

> "How can you call yourself 'pro-life' and support laws that force women to gamble with not only their own lives but their babies' lives? I don't understand the logic."[22]
>
> —Ashley Brandt, a Texas woman denied an abortion in her home state

Statton was turned away from three Oklahoma hospitals before she and her husband decided to drive to neighboring Kansas—180 miles (290 km) away—to get the abortion and save her life. Both worried that Statton's condition might worsen during the arduous car trip before they could get help.

At Oklahoma Children's Hospital, the last facility to deny her care before heading to Kansas, Statton says that staff members refused to perform a surgical abortion unless her condition seriously deteriorated, such as going into cardiac arrest. Statton sued the hospital, arguing that the hospital was required under federal law to provide an abortion in an urgent situation, no matter what the state allowed. She also filed a federal complaint. An investigation of that complaint concluded that Oklahoma Children's

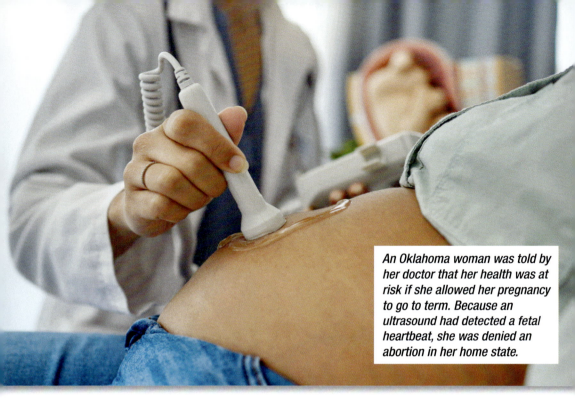

An Oklahoma woman was told by her doctor that her health was at risk if she allowed her pregnancy to go to term. Because an ultrasound had detected a fetal heartbeat, she was denied an abortion in her home state.

Hospital had not violated federal law. Stratton disagrees. "Oklahoma's laws nearly killed me. . . . No one ever thinks they need an abortion, but I am living proof that abortion is healthcare. It's not safe to be pregnant in Oklahoma. With this complaint, I want to make sure that no one else has to suffer the way I did."[23]

Statton says she suffered emotional, financial, and physical trauma from her experience. Her lawsuit caused her and her family to relive the ordeal. It is certainly not something that any woman wants to go through, but Statton was lucky in one way: she had the ability and the means to arrange for an out-of-state abortion. Other families lack the resources necessary to travel to an abortion-friendly state for their procedure. Families in this situation have little choice—which can be devastating all on its own.

Thirteen-year-old Ashley (not her real name) was happily playing outside in the fall of 2022 when a stranger dragged her from her front yard, raped her on the side of the house—and impregnated her. By the time the facts came out a few months later, it was too late for Ashley to seek an abortion in her home state

23

Clarifying Abortion Law

Texas has some of the strictest abortion laws in the nation. Nearly all abortions are banned, but the state does allow abortions for medical exceptions. But the language of the law is posing problems. Experts disagree about what those exceptions are, when they apply, and how doctors should interpret them. In January 2024, attorneys Steve and Amy Bresnan filed a petition with the Texas Medical Board (TMB) asking for more straightforward guidance concerning those exceptions. "The Legislature, the Governor, the Supreme Court of Texas and physicians have asked for clarity and the TMB has the power to give it. There is no excuse for further delay," Steve Bresnan said. In March, the TMB agreed to consider clarifying the legal wording for those exceptions.

Quoted in Madaleine Rubin, "Texas Medical Board Asked to Issue Guidance on State Abortion Laws," *Texas Tribune*, January 16, 2024. www.texastribune.org.

of Mississippi, which has some of the strictest abortion laws on the books. Searching in other states, Ashley's family found that the closest abortion clinic that would take her was in Chicago—a nine-hour trip by car. But Ashley's family did not have the money to cover the procedure and the road trip. The following August, just before starting seventh grade, Ashley gave birth to a baby boy. On top of homework assignments and school projects, Ashley now spends her days and nights raising her child. Reflecting on what had happened to her daughter, Ashley's mother said, "This situation hurts the most because it was an innocent child doing what children do, playing outside, and it was my child. It still hurts, and is going to always hurt."[24]

> "This situation hurts the most because it was an innocent child doing what children do, playing outside, and it was my child. It still hurts, and is going to always hurt."[24]
>
> —Mother of a thirteen-year-old rape victim

Surging Demand, Fewer Choices

In the year following the *Dobbs* ruling, states reacted swiftly with their new authority to regulate abortion. According to the Guttmacher Institute, fourteen states banned abortion and another seven states restricted access to abortion. In contrast, twenty-two states and the District of Columbia took steps to safeguard the procedure. As citizens mobilize and legal challenges are filed on both sides of the debate, these numbers will likely change. Without question, the *Dobbs* decision made obtaining an abortion more difficult, but it did not stop abortions in this country. Data from the Guttmacher Institute shows a dramatic upswing in the total number of abortions performed in 2023 compared to 2020. Following the *Dobbs* ruling, for example, New Mexico (where abortion is legal) saw a 61 percent increase in the average monthly number of abortions. New Mexico shares a border with Texas and Oklahoma, both states that have severely restricted abortions. Likewise, Illinois saw a 33 percent jump. It shares borders with Missouri and Kentucky, two more states that have enacted abortion restrictions. As the *New York Times* reported in September 2023, "Abortions rose in nearly every state where the procedure remains legal, but the change was most visible in states bordering those with total abortion bans."[25]

New Mexico, where abortion is legal, has seen a huge increase in the number of women seeking abortions. Many come from the neighboring states of Texas and Oklahoma, both of which have severely restricted abortion.

The repercussions of the *Dobbs* decision are spreading across US society, sometimes in unexpected ways. Abortion was once considered a common, available, and relatively routine form of reproductive health care. But as the procedure has become endangered or even out of reach, it is affecting family planning. Now, some young women are feeling pressure *not* to have children. In a poll by All In Together and Echelon Insights, a third of women aged eighteen to thirty-nine "said they or someone they know personally has 'decided not to get pregnant due to concerns about managing pregnancy-related medical emergencies.'"[26] In other words, a sizable segment of women in their childbearing years are rethinking their decision to start or add to their family because they are fearful that *Dobbs* robs them of the health care and support network they require. "Abortion bans make pregnancy less safe and women are acutely aware of the consequence of restricting access to reproductive health care in

An 1864 Abortion Ban Is Revived

A 160-year-old law in Arizona is the basis for regulating abortion in the state. The law was passed in 1864, before Arizona became a state and before women had the right to vote. The Civil War–era law had stayed dormant for decades as new laws limiting abortion in Arizona went into effect—but it was never taken off the books. In April 2024, the Arizona Supreme Court upheld the law. The law bans nearly all abortions except in instances when the mother's life is in danger, but it does not allow exceptions for rape or incest. Anyone successfully prosecuted under the law could face a prison term of two to five years. An effort by Democrats in the Arizona House of Representatives to overturn the law failed. "I will continue to call on the legislature to do its job and repeal the law. A law from 1864 written by 27 men cannot be allowed to govern the lives of millions of Arizona women," Governor Katie Hobbs said in a statement. A bill to repeal the 1864 ban subsequently passed the House and then the Senate in May, before heading to the governor for her eventual signature.

Quoted in Liliana Salgado and Daniel Trotta, "Arizona Republicans Uphold 1864 Abortion Ban, Democrats Still Seek Repeal," Reuters, April 18, 2024. www.reuters.com.

their own lives,"[27] explains Alexis McGill Johnson, chief executive officer (CEO) of Planned Parenthood.

The *Dobbs* decision has put pressure on women that they have not felt in almost fifty years. In states where abortion is banned or severely restricted, women who need or want the procedure face enormous obstacles. Their local doctors and hospitals, used to performing abortions routinely, are hesitant to do so for fear of being prosecuted. Women who desperately need an abortion often have to wait and endure unnecessary pain until they finally receive proper help. Other women have traveled to states where abortion is permitted. Still others, who could not travel for an abortion, have been forced to give birth regardless of their needs or wants. Whether it was a thirteen-year-old girl who got pregnant by rape or a twenty-five-year-old Oklahoma woman who was turned down by three area hospitals for an abortion to save her life, the health care of women in the United States is in jeopardy. The struggle to alleviate this threat and to restore a woman's right to choose—without obstacles—shows no signs of letting up.

> "Abortion bans make pregnancy less safe and women are acutely aware of the consequence of restricting access to reproductive health care in their own lives."[27]
>
> —Alexis McGill Johnson, CEO of Planned Parenthood

CHAPTER THREE

Medical Professionals Under Fire

When abortion was legal under *Roe*, doctors were free to perform the procedure without undue fear of prosecution. No matter the reason for the abortion, the law respected the doctor's judgment and the woman's (or the couple's) wishes. The *Dobbs* ruling radically changed this situation. States now have the power to decide whether to allow abortions within their borders and, if so, under what conditions.

> "Sometimes I feel that I am not able to fulfill the Hippocratic Oath that I took when I graduated from medical school. Because sometimes, not providing abortion care is actually doing harm."[28]
>
> —Dr. Rachel Weinerman, an ob-gyn at Case Western Reserve University

In the immediate aftermath of *Dobbs*, many states have imposed tighter restrictions on abortion or even outlawed the procedure. Many health care providers in these states say the new restrictions have affected their ability to care for their patients. In Ohio, where an abortion ban went into effect and then was put on hold by a state court, doctors expressed their frustration about treating their maternity patients. "Sometimes I feel that I am not able to fulfill the Hippocratic Oath that I took when I graduated from medical school. Because sometimes, not providing abortion care is actually doing harm,"[28] says Dr. Rachel Weinerman, an obstetrician-gynecologist (ob-gyn) at Case Western Reserve University in Cleveland.

This view is not universal, however. Some medical providers in these same states say the new laws that restrict or ban abortions have not affected quality of care. On the contrary, they argue that the right to abortion has had a negative impact on women's health. "Abortion significantly increases the risk for depression, anxiety, substance abuse and suicidal ideation and behavior—even when compared to women with unintended pregnancies who carried to term,"[29] says Dr. Christina Francis, an ob-gyn in Indiana and head of the American Association of Pro-Life Obstetricians and Gynecologists.

> "Abortion significantly increases the risk for depression, anxiety, substance abuse and suicidal ideation and behavior—even when compared to women with unintended pregnancies who carried to term."[29]
>
> —Dr. Christina Francis, an ob-gyn in Indiana and head of the American Association of Pro-Life Obstetricians and Gynecologists

Doctors Risk Prosecution

Despite the different perspectives within the medical profession, fear and uncertainty have become a reality for many doctors and other health care professionals who provide reproductive services.

Some doctors say that quality of care has not been affected by new abortion restrictions. Many others express frustration, saying the new laws have hurt their ability to care for pregnant patients.

Before *Dobbs*, abortions were considered a fairly routine procedure. Women could make appointments at any number of clinics in states all across the country. In most cases, an appointment for an abortion performed by a doctor could be obtained within a few days. For abortions done early in a pregnancy, the actual procedure usually took about ten minutes. Abortions done after sixteen weeks could take twice as long. In both cases, the office visit also entailed a pelvic exam and about an hour in the recovery room after the procedure. Complications sometimes occurred, but not often.

Since *Dobbs*, in many states, abortions are no longer routine. Some doctors are withholding care until they consult with attorneys, jeopardizing women's health. In a June 2023 survey released by KFF, a nonprofit organization that covers health policy research, 40 percent of ob-gyns across the country said "they've felt constrained in their ability to provide care during pregnancy-related medical emergencies."[30]

Even in cases when abortion is necessary to save the life of the mother, many doctors say they are fearful of performing an abortion because of the threat of criminal prosecution. According to Dr. Katie McHugh, who provides abortions in Indiana, "There is no way that I would risk my personal freedom and jail time for providing medical care. I would love to show my children that I am brave in the world, but our society will not allow me to be a civil-disobedient citizen in the way that some of these articles suggest, because I would be imprisoned, I would be fined, I would lose my license."[31]

In Tennessee, for example, abortion is banned except to save the life of the mother. But the law also requires an "affirmative defense." So if the doctor's actions resulted in criminal charges, that doctor would have to prove in court that the procedure was necessary and met the state's legal standards, according to Metropolitan Nashville's Law Director. Affirmative defense requirements also exist in Idaho and Missouri. In September 2023, a lawsuit was filed on behalf of three women and abortion providers by the Center for Reproductive Rights against the state of Tennessee

A Mountain of Paperwork

All doctors must document visits and prescribed treatments. Asking patients to sign consent forms for certain procedures is also not unusual. But North Carolina has taken this to a new level, putting time-consuming requirements in place after *Dobbs*. Under a law passed in 2023, no doctor can perform an abortion before obtaining twenty separate signed consent forms from the patient. One of these forms gives patients the right to sue the doctor if they feel that the doctor misled them or pressured them into having an abortion. "As a physician who takes an oath to do no harm, that feels like a punch to the gut," says Dr. Brittany Davidson, an associate professor of obstetrics and gynecology at Duke Health.

Before *Dobbs*, women were also required by the state to undergo a counseling session seventy-two hours before an abortion procedure, either over the phone or online. Now doctors are required to conduct these sessions in person. This change adds to overbooked schedules, makes more work for office staff, and often delays patient appointments.

Quoted in Stacy Weiner, "The Fallout of *Dobbs* on the Field of OB-GYN," AAMCNews, August 23, 2023. www.aamc.org.

over its abortion ban. The outcome will likely have a major impact on the state's affirmative defense requirement. "The abortion ban directly regulates what care [physicians] can and cannot provide their patients and it affects them by threatening them with imprisonment, fines and loss of their medical license if they violate the law,"[32] said Marc Hearron, the center's attorney.

Some doctors in South Dakota say they have been put in an impossible situation. State law prohibits abortions from being performed, except for narrow exceptions where the health of a pregnant woman could be endangered. Under the law, doctors may use their best judgment in determining that an abortion is needed. However, if a court or prosecutor disagrees with the doctor's determination, that doctor could be charged with a felony. "It's impossible to itemize every situation where ending a pregnancy might be necessary to protect the health of the mother, and we shouldn't have to demonstrate evidence of imminent death to care for these patients without fear of a felony charge,"[33] says Dr. Erica Schipper, a Sioux Falls ob-gyn and former chair of the South Dakota chapter of the American College of Obstetricians and Gynecologists.

Fear and Patient Care

Carmen Broesder believes that she was denied the care she desperately needed because her doctors feared punishment for unintentionally violating state law. In 2022, the thirty-five-year-old and her boyfriend were already the parents of a little girl in the state of Idaho. Eager for another child, they were delighted when Broesder learned she was pregnant with the couple's second child. In early December, at six weeks, Broesder experienced excessive bleeding and pain. She knew these to be clear signs that she was miscarrying. She went to the emergency room, where she expected to undergo a dilation and curettage procedure, commonly called a D&C. The procedure is relatively routine and is performed to clean out tissue from a woman's uterus and to stop blood loss when a woman miscarries. But the emergency room doctors refused to do the D&C, which is also commonly used in abortions.

Abortion is completely banned in Idaho. There is a narrow exception in Idaho if the mother's life is in danger, but that could be open to interpretation in a court of law. "Hospital administrators are telling us that the lack of clarity in Idaho's legal environment regarding maternal health care has created uncertainty and fear,"[34] says Brian Whitlock, CEO of the Idaho Hospital Association.

Broesder suspected that the doctors' refusal had more to do with their fear of the state's wide-ranging restrictions and less with whether she actually needed the procedure for health reasons. When she pressed her doctors on why they did not do a D&C, it became clear that they did not want to chance being prosecuted under Idaho law. During a visit with a doctor who refused to perform an abortion, Broesder made an audio recording of their conversation that confirmed her suspicions. "Regarding D&C, there is some confusion—not confusion—some trepidation regarding, kind of, Idaho's new abortion law,"[35] the doctor says in the recording.

Broesder endured intense pain and continued to bleed for days. Still, she could not find a doctor who would grant her request for a D&C or prescribe pain medication. When an exam revealed part of an embryo lodged in the narrow end of her uterus, doctors performed a surgical procedure to remove it. They sent Broesder home with the medication misoprostol, which would bring on labor and cause an abortion. Her ordeal, which she recorded and posted in a series of videos on TikTok, lasted nineteen days and left an indelible impression on her. "I did not deserve to have to beg for my life for eight days and nobody else does either,"[36] Broesder says.

> "I did not deserve to have to beg for my life for eight days and nobody else does either."[36]
>
> —Carmen Broesder, an Idaho resident denied medically necessary abortion care

The Cost of Speaking Up

States that border each other and have different abortion laws can cause unforeseen problems for health care providers. Dr. Caitlin Bernard is an Indianapolis ob-gyn. Three days after the *Dobbs* decision in June 2022, Bernard was contacted by a doctor in neighboring Ohio who treated child abuse cases. The doctor told her that the family of a ten-year-old Ohio girl who had been raped and impregnated was in the office. The girl was a little over six weeks pregnant—past Ohio's abortion ban limit, but within Indiana's twenty-two-week allowance. The doctor asked whether the girl could be referred to Bernard, and she agreed. An article in the *Indianapolis Star* broke the story of the girl's situation and revealed Bernard as the doctor who performed the abortion. Various media outlets pressed Bernard for more details, but she refused to provide them.

When word got out that Bernard had performed the abortion, Indiana's attorney general, Todd Rokita, reported her to the Indiana Medical Licensing Board. He urged them to investigate Bernard's actions. He did not claim that she performed an illegal abortion. Instead, he accused her of violating the patient's privacy by speaking about the situation publicly. Although Bernard did

Indiana's attorney general was reprimanded for his public comments about Dr. Caitlin Bernard (pictured in March 2024), an Indianapolis ob-gyn who performed a legal abortion on a ten-year-old rape victim from Ohio.

join a march to Indiana's state capitol to speak out against abortion restrictions, she maintained that she did nothing wrong in the way she spoke about her ten-year-old patient.

The Indiana Medical Licensing Board disagreed. It censured Bernard and fined her three thousand dollars. More than five hundred doctors in Indiana signed and sent an open letter of protest to the board. It read, in part, "To punish a physician for fulfilling her professional and legal obligations sets a very dangerous and chilling precedent for each of us, regardless of medical specialty."[37] Upon further examination, Indiana University Health, where Bernard practices, concluded that she did not violate any privacy standards. Later, the Indiana Supreme Court determined that Rokita's comments violated ethics rules and reprimanded him. Bernard says that "none of this should have happened in a sane world. The problem is that I didn't realize we weren't operating in a sane world."[38]

Doctors Pushed to the Limit

Adding to the difficulties encountered by doctors who are trying to care for their patients is a huge surge in demand in states where abortion is still legal. Medical providers in these states are stretched thin. At the University of New Mexico's Center for Reproductive Health, 20 percent of patients typically came from out of state before *Dobbs*. After *Dobbs* went into effect, that number jumped to 80 percent, with many coming from the more restrictive neighboring state of Texas. "We have already reached capacity,"[39] says Dr. Amber Truehart, medical director at the center. Phone inquiries have reached critical proportions too. Hope Clinic for Women in Illinois was typically receiving an average of 170 phone calls per day. On the day the *Dobbs* ruling was announced, the clinic logged more than 600 calls. Hope Clinic staff are working ten to twelve hours a day to handle the crush of patients—exhausting medical and support personnel.

Doctors Forced to Relocate

Dr. Kylie Cooper, a maternal-fetal specialist, moved to Boise, Idaho, in 2008 with her husband, two small children, and a burning desire to help her patients. She eagerly took on complex cases or pregnancies where complications might develop. Her patients adored her, and she was proud to be delivering excellent medical care. "We just had a good life. We had no plans to leave," Cooper said during an Associated Press interview. After the *Dobbs* ruling in 2022, however, Idaho banned almost all abortions. Now, any doctor who performs an abortion risks being prosecuted, fined, and jailed.

Cooper found herself spending valuable time consulting with attorneys—time taken away from her patients—before making medical decisions. In April 2023, Cooper reluctantly closed her practice and moved to Minnesota, where abortion is legal. She and her family loved Idaho, but the threat of a prison sentence and of depriving her children of their mother was too great to bear. One of Cooper's patients commented, "I'm just really sad. She was so kind. She changed our lives. I don't blame her for leaving. But it sucks for everyone here."

Quoted in Laura Ungar, "Why Some Doctors Stay in US States with Restrictive Abortion Laws and Others Leave," Associated Press, June 22, 2023. https://apnews.com.

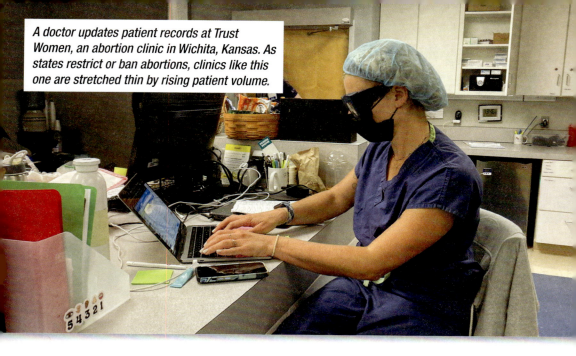

A doctor updates patient records at Trust Women, an abortion clinic in Wichita, Kansas. As states restrict or ban abortions, clinics like this one are stretched thin by rising patient volume.

At the Boulder Valley Women's Health Center in Colorado, the center has had to extend its hours to handle the patient surge. The center has seen the number of abortions double. Often, only one physician is available, with little to no time for a break or to eat lunch. "I hate to turn people away,"[40] Dr. Kelly Peters, the center's medical director, says. Trust Women, a Wichita, Kansas–based abortion clinic, was already at capacity when it saw its patient volume surge. "We feel kind of powerless. We all just don't know what to do right now,"[41] says clinic director Ashley Brink.

The *Dobbs* decision has changed how reproductive health care is practiced in the United States. Many doctors say the new laws are so rigid or unclear that they fear being prosecuted, fined or losing their medical license even for procedures that have traditionally been viewed as routine. Other doctors argue that *Dobbs* is a long overdue step forward in preventing the deaths of innocent fetuses. For women who want or need abortions and cannot get them, these disagreements and restrictions can have life-altering consequences. In the opinion of Dr. Stella Dantas, the president-elect of the American College of Obstetricians and Gynecologists, "This isn't an issue about abortion. This is an issue about access to comprehensive obstetric and gynecologic care."[42]

CHAPTER FOUR

The Quest to End Abortion

The *Dobbs* decision, affirming that there is no constitutional right to abortion, represents a monumental victory for the pro-life movement. Overturning the 1973 Supreme Court ruling that legalized abortion had been a clear and consistent goal for almost fifty years. But rather than viewing *Dobbs* as an end in itself, the movement sees it as a stepping stone to a far more ambitious objective: outlawing abortion all across the country.

Younger Antiabortion Crusaders

Energized by *Dobbs*, pro-life groups have not wasted any time in capitalizing on this historic court ruling. They want to keep the momentum going to reach their ultimate goal of an abortion-free America. Older organizations, such as National Right to Life, have been instrumental in this fight. They have been joined by a new wave of antiabortion activists who are more vocal, more assertive, and possibly even more influential. Notably, Students for Life of America (SFLA) and its president, Kristan Hawkins, are among the leading forces in what they and others often refer to as "the post-*Roe* generation." Hawkins launched SFLA in August 2006. The organization says it now has more than fourteen hundred pro-life student groups on school campuses in all fifty states, and it claims on its website to have trained at least 180,000 advocates. Although there are no concrete figures

Kristan Hawkins (celebrating the one-year anniversary of the Dobbs ruling at a June 2023 rally in Washington, DC) founded Students for Life of America in 2006. Hawkins is among a new wave of influential antiabortion activists.

about the age and demographic makeup of the post-*Roe* generation, thirty-eight-year-old Hawkins epitomizes this new group of antiabortion crusaders.

Hawkins's outlook, her thinking, and her strategies have infused the movement with renewed life. During the almost fifty years since the *Roe* decision, the pro-life movement had notched some victories that chipped away at abortion protections. For some in the movement, overturning *Roe* seemed like a far-distant reality, but not to Hawkins. She firmly believed that she would live to see the repeal of *Roe* during her lifetime. Many in the pro-life movement were shocked but ecstatic when *Roe* fell. Hawkins, though, seemed unsurprised by the ruling. She had, after all, been an ardent opponent of abortion and had been building an organization and training a nationwide army of activists since 2006—ready and eager to take on pro-choice advocates. The conservative majority on the US Supreme Court was also most receptive to the position she stood for. "For Students for Life, [*Dobbs*] didn't change anything. This is why I built Students for Life, to be a post-*Roe* organization, to have trained activists . . . in all 50 states. I think *Dobbs* just sped up the urgency and the number of fights,"[43] Hawkins said in an August 2023 interview in the *New York Times*.

The stated goal of SFLA is nothing less than the abolition of abortion. In that respect, it is not unlike other, older pro-life organizations. Yet SFLA seems to be taking the fight to a new level, with an unbridled enthusiasm that is reinvigorating the abortion debate. "What has changed is they are willing to say the quiet part out loud. They are willing to be publicly extreme,"[44] says Elisabeth Smith of the Center for Reproductive Rights. To that end, it is employing a number of strategies to achieve its goal, such as pushing to grant legal protection to life starting at conception. The group also favors defunding the so-called "abortion industry," such as blocking all taxpayer dollars from going to organizations such as Planned Parenthood. Planned Parenthood provides a range of health care services to women, with only about 3 percent of its services related to abortions. The government partially reimburses Planned Parenthood for these services. SFLA objects to using the money from taxpayers to support this work.

Since *Dobbs* empowered individual states to set abortion regulations, Hawkins has been working diligently to urge state legislators around the country to pass stringent antiabortion measures. For example, SFLA is fighting for an "early abortion" standard—essentially, legislation that restricts abortion after six weeks. In April 2023, Florida governor Ron DeSantis signed a bill that did just that—a victory that Hawkins attributes to her campaign.

Hawkins and SFLA do more than simply lobby for passage of more restrictive abortion laws. The group has also written and provided lawmakers with templates that they can use to draft antiabortion bills.

Lawmakers Respond

The *Dobbs* decision also galvanized current and former federal officeholders who oppose abortion. Although the ruling gave states the power to regulate abortion, it did not prohibit Congress from enacting laws that would set the standard for the nation as a whole. As with any federal law, passage would require a minimum number of votes from both houses of Congress as well as signature by the president. Neither branch of government shows signs of overcoming the obstacles needed to craft such legislation.

Despite this dynamic, former vice president Mike Pence has said that he supports a federal abortion ban at six weeks of pregnancy. And he urged fellow Republicans running for office in 2024 to support a minimum fifteen-week federal ban. In 2022, South Carolina senator Lindsay Graham also proposed a new nationwide abortion law. If enacted, this law would ban abortion after fifteen weeks, with exclusions for rape, incest, and risks to the mother's health.

Banning Abortions by Pill

Since the *Dobbs* ruling, abortion opponents have mostly focused on blocking abortion services that women obtain in person at clinics. But in-person abortions are no longer the most common form of abortion. More than half of all abortions done today take place at home with the help of two drugs: mifepristone and misoprostol. Approved by the Food and Drug Administration (FDA) in 2000, mifepristone became available with a doctor's prescription at select pharmacies in states where abortion is legal starting in March 2024. This form of abortion, known as medication abortion, has become the focus of individuals and groups trying to eliminate abortion.

Medication abortion relies on this two-drug combination. Mifepristone works by preventing the fertilized egg from attaching to the wall of the uterus within the first seventy days of a pregnancy. The drug induces a menstrual cycle, causing the fertilized egg to be expelled from the uterus. Misoprostol, the second drug, is taken afterward to clear the uterus of pregnancy-related tissue, thereby ending the pregnancy.

> "I believe all life is sacred and that every individual, including the unborn, should be treated with dignity and compassion."[45]
>
> —Mark Gordon, governor of Wyoming

Hawkins and SFLA have zeroed in on medication abortions as the next front in their efforts to eliminate abortion in America. Their efforts have met with some success. In Wyoming, SFLA members spent two years actively lobbying and working with state representatives to craft legislation that would ban the sale of abortion pills. In March 2023, the governor signed the bill into law making it a crime—punishable by $9,000 fines and up to six months in jail—for doctors to prescribe these pills. "I have a strong record of protecting the lives of the unborn, as well as their mothers. I believe all life is sacred and that every individual, including the unborn, should be treated with dignity and compassion,"[45] Governor Mark Gordon said.

Abortion opponents are fighting retail pharmacy chains Walgreens and CVS, which are dispensing the abortion pill mifepristone in some states. Protesters rally outside the Illinois headquarters of Walgreens in February 2023.

On another front, SFLA is taking its fight against medication abortion directly to local drugstores. In January 2023, the FDA gave retail pharmacies permission to dispense mifepristone with a doctor's prescription. In March 2024, CVS and Walgreens announced plans to start offering the pill in a few of their stores at first and then more broadly. The new policy will make it easier and more convenient for women to terminate their pregnancies. Abortion opponents have boycotted these pharmacy chains and protested in front of stores. Hawkins, who has referred to CVS as "the nation's largest abortion vendor,"[46] and SFLA are working to remove abortion pills from retail pharmacies such as CVS, Walgreens, and Rite Aid.

SFLA is far from alone in trying to eliminate chemical abortions. After the 2022 *Dobbs* decision, antiabortion groups calling themselves the Alliance for Hippocratic Medicine sued the FDA over its approval of mifepristone, hoping to take it off the market in the United States. In August 2023, a federal appeals court panel ruled that "mifepristone should remain legal in the United States but with significant restrictions on patients' access to it."[47] Before this ruling, patients had greater access to the pill because health care providers who were not doctors could prescribe it, and patients could get the pill without having to visit a health care provider in person. The court's decision would prohibit mifepristone from being sent through the mail or prescribed via a telemedicine provider. The US Justice Department appealed to the Supreme Court, which heard arguments in March 2024. A ruling was expected by summer 2024.

Antiabortion Groups Push Forward

Feeling the momentum of the moment, antiabortion groups are moving ahead on other issues. One group, Live Action, is pushing for a halt to all federal funds to family planning groups that offer abortion services. A group like Planned Parenthood, for example, which received about $148 million between 2019 and 2021 from federal sources other than Medicaid or Medicare. These federal funds, made up of money collected from citizens through taxes, are prohibited from being used for abortions, except in cases of

The Ultimate Penalty

In January 2023, a Republican state representative named Rob Harris proposed a bill to the South Carolina General Assembly. Called the South Carolina Prenatal Equal Protection Act of 2023, the bill would have made anyone who had an abortion subject to a minimum prison term of thirty years—or death. The bill expanded the definition of *person* under the criminal code to include a fetus at any stage of development, giving it equal protection under the law. The bill made no exceptions for rape or incest, but it did have allowances if the woman's life or health were in danger.

Twenty-four Republicans lawmakers initially supported the bill, but other Republicans believed the punishment was too extreme. Republican representative Nancy Mace commented, "To see this debate go to the dark places, the dark edges, where it has gone on both sides of the aisle has been deeply disturbing to me as a woman, as a female legislator, as a mom, and as a victim of rape. This debate ought to be a bipartisan debate where we balance the rights of women and we balance the right to life." By March 2023, at least nine Republican supporters had changed their position.

Quoted in Ken Tran, "South Carolina GOP Lawmakers Consider Death Penalty for People Who Have Abortions," *USA Today*, March 14, 2023. www.usatoday.com.

rape, incest, or when the mother's life is endangered—exceptions that Live Action does not support. Lila Rose, founder of Live Action, contends that "there are truly no medical situations in which abortion, the direct, intentional killing of a preborn baby, is necessary to save a woman's life."[48]

Rose started Live Action in 2003 when she was only fifteen years old. "I discovered that there were 3,000 abortions every day at the time and I felt convinced that something had to be done,"[49] Rose explains. Live Action gained notoriety after Rose went undercover at two Planned Parenthood clinics and recorded controversial videos. Posing as a fifteen-year-old impregnated by an older man, Rose claims that Planned Parenthood staff told her to lie about her age so they would not have to report this as a case of statutory rape to the authorities. Planned Parenthood denied

> "There are truly no medical situations in which abortion, the direct, intentional killing of a preborn baby, is necessary to save a woman's life."[48]
>
> —Lila Rose, founder and president of Live Action

Rose's claims, saying the videos were edited to reflect poorly on the clinics. Today, Live Action claims to reach over 6 million followers on social media and to provide news and content that reaches 70 million people every month.

Rose's group is also fighting for laws that would recognize the personhood of every fetus. Supporters of this idea are pushing for either a constitutional amendment that grants rights to a fetus or an official recognition that they already enjoy personhood status under the Fourteenth Amendment of the US Constitution. The amendment, in part, prohibits states from denying "to any person within its jurisdiction the equal protection of the laws."[50]

The amendment was ratified three years after the end of the Civil War to protect newly freed slaves. Rose argues that such

Lila Rose (speaking at a 2019 event) founded the antiabortion group Live Action. Rose and her organization are pushing for a halt to all federal funds to family planning groups that offer abortion services.

Legal Rights for the Unborn

At a rally of pro-life supporters at the Lincoln Memorial on the one-year anniversary of the *Dobbs* decision, both Kristan Hawkins of Students for Life of America and Lila Rose of Live Action addressed the crowd. Although they celebrated new abortion restrictions that had been enacted, the fight was far from over. They argued that life begins at conception, entitling every fetus to equal protection under the law, "not because of what state their mother resides in or if they are perceived to be convenient or the circumstances of their conception," Hawkins said. Rose had a similar message: "When it comes to preborn children we have failed to extend these protections." Such a view does not appear to be shared by a majority of citizens. A KFF poll released in March 2024 found that two-thirds of the public favored a law guaranteeing a federal right to abortion. The debate over whether and when a fetus should be granted legal status does not look like it will be settled soon.

Quoted in Lauretta Brown, "Pro-Lifers Celebrate *Roe*'s Demise, Push for Nationwide Protection for the Unborn," Catholic News Agency, June 25, 2023. www.catholicnewsagency.com.

protection under the law should apply to the unborn as well. "Let me speak with one clear message: We demand equal protection for pre-born children. California, New York, states across our country are violating our 14th Amendment by preying upon our most vulnerable pre-born brothers and sisters."[51]

Now that *Roe* has been overturned, the antiabortion movement is pressing to outlaw all abortions in the United States with no exceptions. Not everyone in the movement agrees with this position. Some pro-life supporters feel that certain allowances should be made, such as when the mother's life is in jeopardy. Nevertheless, organizations such as SFLA are fighting to close access to abortion in every way, such as pressuring drugstores to stop dispensing abortion-inducing medication. They are working closely with government officials to pass laws to eliminate abortion forever and completely. "I will be that person who's never satisfied until we reach that day where no woman feels she has to choose the violence of abortion in order to be a free, equal member of our society, in order to complete her education or reach her career goals,"[52] Hawkins says.

CHAPTER FIVE

Efforts to Restore Abortion Rights

When the Supreme Court overturned *Roe v. Wade*, it did more than energize individuals and groups that oppose abortion. It also reinvigorated efforts by individuals and groups who believe abortions must be legal, safe, and available to women who want or need them. These efforts have included proposed laws at the federal level, protections at the state level, legal challenges to restrictive laws, and ballot initiatives. Just as *Dobbs* energized pro-life groups, the pro-choice movement has been equally galvanized by the Supreme Court decision. Groups, advocates for women's rights, and individual citizens are fighting to overturn abortion restrictions, restore abortion freedoms, and empower women to be in charge of their own reproductive decisions. These efforts are playing out on multiple fronts.

Expanding Legal Protections

Members of Congress who support abortion rights have introduced bills to protect doctors and patients nationwide. Among these bills is one that would eliminate the threat of prosecution against doctors who determine that an abortion is the best course of action for a patient. Called the Let Doctors Provide Reproductive Health Care Act, the measure would safeguard doctors and anyone who assists them in providing abortion care from criminal liability. To that end, the bill would prohibit an individual, an organization, or even a state government from interfering in any way with lawful reproductive health care services. Funds would also be made available to health care providers for any legal issues that might arise and for enhanced security protection. "This bill protects women and doctors from unjust prosecution and ensures that patients and their doctors are the ones making personal medical decisions, not the government,"[53] says the bill's cosponsor, Washington congresswoman and pediatrician Kim Schrier.

Another proposed bill, called the Women's Health Protection Act of 2023, would guarantee women the health care options they want, especially abortion, without obstacle. Among other things, it would prohibit waiting periods—the time between a woman having a counseling session with her health care provider and the abortion procedure. Many states require at least twenty-four hours to elapse between appointments, but others, such as Arkansas and Missouri, have mandatory seventy-two-hour waiting periods. In states where counseling must be done in person and not over the phone or by video chat, women have the added burden of making two

Hundreds of people take part in a pro-choice rally in Chicago on the day the Supreme Court overturned Roe v. Wade. Pro-choice groups and individuals are working to restore abortion access on multiple fronts.

> "As we navigate a post-*Dobbs* world and continue to face relentless attacks on our freedom and bodily autonomy, let me make it plain: abortion care is routine medical care and a fundamental human right."[54]
>
> —Ayanna Pressley, congresswoman from Massachusetts

trips to their provider. Policies vary from state to state about what must be covered in the counseling sessions. According to the Guttmacher Institute, in August 2023 five states required women to be told that personhood begins at conception, fourteen states had information about the ability of the fetus to feel pain, and twenty-eight states about the risks of abortion.

It would also eliminate procedures that most doctors say are medically unnecessary for a first-trimester abortion, such as an ultrasound, but that several states require before a woman can obtain an abortion. Those who support abortion rights consider these impediments unwarranted intrusions into their health care decisions. "As we navigate a post-*Dobbs* world and continue to face relentless attacks on our freedom and bodily autonomy, let me make it plain: abortion care is routine medical care and a fundamental human right,"[54] asserts Congresswoman Ayanna Pressley of Massachusetts.

Besides restricting abortion within their boundaries, some states want to control a woman's access to abortion even in states where it was legal. Two weeks after the *Dobbs* decision was handed down, more than thirty senators in Congress introduced legislation to counter this obstacle. Called the Freedom to Travel for Health Care Act, the bill would bar anyone—including government officials—from interfering with or hindering a person's right to leave a state to obtain an abortion. Despite the flurry of bills put forward, Congress remains deeply divided on this issue, and political experts say it is unlikely that any federal abortion laws will pass anytime soon.

Fighting on the State Level

While pro-choice members of Congress have been trying to craft and pass laws that would protect the right to abortion nationwide, elected officeholders in states have also been taking action. In Illinois, for example, Governor J.B. Pritzker launched Think Big America, a social welfare organization whose central focus is protecting abortion rights in states where they are under siege. Launched in October 2023, Think Big America supports state ballot initiatives that would codify abortion rights into law. A billionaire businessman, Pritzker is funding Think Big America out of his own pocket, donating money from his personal fortune and staff members from his office. For the November 2024 elections, for example, he gave $250,000 to a coalition of groups supporting a ballot measure in Arizona that would enshrine the right to abortion in the state constitution.

Efforts to restrict access to abortion pills have also caught the attention of elected officials in pro-choice states. To counter this trend, New York had begun to stockpile abortion pills so that medication abortions would not be interrupted. The state

Challenging Texas's Abortion Law

Amanda Zurawski and her husband were excited at the prospect of becoming new parents. But during the second trimester of Zurawski's pregnancy, her cervical membranes ruptured. Her health care team told her that the fetus could not survive and that her own life was in danger. They also told Zurawski that they were powerless to perform an abortion because she did not qualify under Texas law. "Somehow, the medical help I needed to alleviate the horrific inevitability of losing my beloved child 22 weeks early could have been considered illegal," Zurawski says.

Within a few days, Zurawski's blood pressure plummeted and her temperature spiked. She contracted a life-threatening blood infection. Doctors stabilized her just long enough for Zurawski to deliver her daughter—who was stillborn as expected. Zurawski's condition deteriorated immediately thereafter. She spent several days in critical condition while doctors fought to save her life. "An abortion would have prevented the unnecessary harm and suffering that I endured," Zurawski says. "I needed an abortion to protect my life. . . . No one should be forced to remain pregnant against their will for any reason, emergency or no emergency." Zurawski is now the lead plaintiff in a lawsuit opposing Texas's near-total abortion ban.

Amanda Zurawski, "Testimony of Amanda Zurawski Before the Senate Judiciary Committee: 'The Assault on Reproductive Rights in a Post-*Dobbs* America,'" US Senate Committee on the Judiciary, April 26, 2023. www.judiciary.senate.gov.

> "In New York, we remain committed to ensuring abortion remains safe, accessible, and legal."[55]
>
> —Kathy Hochul, governor of New York

also passed a law to protect doctors from prosecution when they prescribe abortion pills to patients who live in states where abortion is prohibited. "In New York, we remain committed to ensuring abortion remains safe, accessible, and legal,"[55] Governor Kathy Hochul said.

Restricting the availability of these drugs has gone from being a state concern to a national one. In 2023 an antiabortion group convinced a Texas court to override the FDA's approval of the abortion pill mifepristone—even though mifepristone had been used safely for more than twenty years. Shortly thereafter, another federal judge in Washington State handed down a ruling that opposed the Texas injunction. In March 2024, the issue went before the US Supreme Court. The court was being asked to decide whether access to mifepristone—available to patients with a prescription through the mail or by telemedicine—had gone too far.

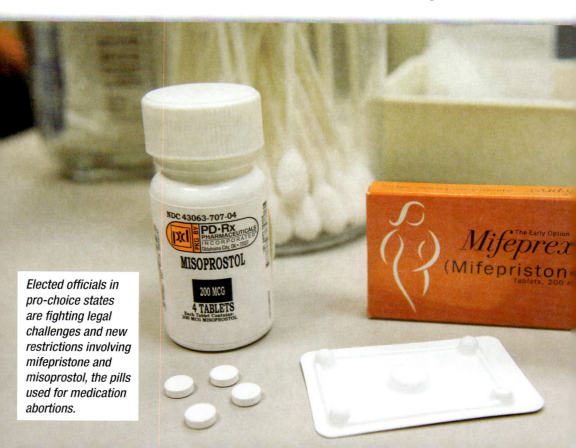

Elected officials in pro-choice states are fighting legal challenges and new restrictions involving mifepristone and misoprostol, the pills used for medication abortions.

In a show of solidarity, twenty-four state attorneys general, led by New York state attorney general Letitia James, filed a brief that supported the FDA's position to remove restrictions on the use and access of mifepristone. In a separate move, Republican governor Phil Scott of Vermont became the first governor in the country to sign a bill into law that would keep access to mifepristone available regardless of the outcome of the FDA lawsuit. "Today, we reaffirm once again that Vermont stands on the side of privacy, personal autonomy and reproductive liberty, and that providers are free to practice without fear,"[56] Scott said.

> "Today, we reaffirm once again that Vermont stands on the side of privacy, personal autonomy and reproductive liberty, and that providers are free to practice without fear."[56]
>
> —Phil Scott, governor of Vermont

More Lawsuits

The debate over restoring abortion rights is also playing out in courtrooms across the country. Pro-choice supporters are making their case in front of judges from district courts to appellate courts to state supreme courts—and sometimes to the US Supreme Court. Individuals who have been hurt by abortion restrictions do not have to stand alone. They can call on the services of groups fighting for women's health care freedom. One such group is the American Civil Liberties Union (ACLU), founded in 1920. As its name implies, the ACLU takes on all types of civil liberties issues, including those dealing with reproductive rights. In December 2023, for example, the ACLU and other groups sued the state of Kentucky over its restrictive abortion ban on behalf of a pregnant woman seeking the procedure.

The Center for Reproductive Rights has also been active in representing people who have been hurt by new restrictions on abortion. In March 2023, for example, the group sued Texas over the "medical emergency" exception policy contained in the state's abortion ban. The exceptions under that law refer to the life and health of the mother—but the center argues that the law's language is contradictory, imprecise, and offers no clear guidance on when the exceptions can be applied. Lack of clarity, the center says, is forcing doctors to hold back medical care out of fear of prosecution. The suit was filed on behalf of five Texas women—who were denied abortions because of state restrictions—and two ob-gyns. The lawsuit contends that the women endured severe, and sometimes life-threatening, complications during their pregnancies—conditions that could have been lessened or resolved if they had received abortions. The lawsuit later grew to include twenty women denied abortion care. In August 2023 a district court blocked the ban and said that doctors could use their own medical judgment when it came to emergency pregnancy situations. The state has appealed to the Texas Supreme Court.

In September 2023, the Center for Reproductive Rights filed a similar lawsuit against the state of Idaho. The center is representing eight patients—who claim they were denied medically necessary abortion care—as well as the Idaho Academy of Family Physicians and four doctors. Again, the center contends that the ban's vague language concerning medical exceptions for abortions is hindering the doctors' ability to provide adequate medical care.

Ballot Initiatives

Ballot initiatives are another tactic being used in the abortion controversy. Ballot initiatives enable citizens to propose amendments to a state's constitution, which are then voted on during the general election by state residents. Ballot initiatives are being used by supporters and opponents of abortion rights.

In several states, pro-life ballot initiatives have been rejected, but pro-choice ballot initiatives have been approved. Most surprising, this has happened in more traditionally conservative states. In Ohio in 2019, for example, Governor Mike DeWine signed into law a six-week ban on abortion, with no exceptions for rape or incest. Although the ban was temporarily paused to allow a legal challenge, the fact that it effectively outlawed abortion in Ohio alarmed pro-choice advocates and compelled them to act.

Missouri Ballot Initiative

A group of abortion rights advocates in Missouri is using the ballot initiative strategy to try to change their state constitution. Missourians for Constitutional Freedom (MCF) consists of groups such as the American Civil Liberties Union and Planned Parenthood as well as individual citizens working to undo Missouri's near-total abortion ban. Abortion is prohibited, even in cases of rape and incest, except for medical emergencies. MCF has proposed an amendment that would severely curtail the government's role in reproductive health and return those decisions to families and their doctors.

MCF was hoping to have enough signatures to qualify the measure for the November 2024 election. Reverend Emily Bowen-Marler, a supporter of the measure, comments that "abortion isn't always cut and dry. For some people, it is an easy decision. For some people, it is an agonizing decision. But either way, it is their decision to make. It is not mine, it is not yours, and it is certainly not the legislators' of Missouri."

Quoted in Missourians for Constitutional Freedom, "Thousands of Missourians Turn Out to Be Among the First to Sign Abortion Petition," press release, February 7, 2024. https://moconstitutionalfreedom.org.

In fall 2023, a consortium of groups—Ohio Physicians for Reproductive Rights, Ohioans for Reproductive Freedom, and others—mobilized to get an initiative, known as Issue 1, before the voters. Issue 1 would add abortion protections to the state constitution. This includes permitting abortions up to fetal viability and letting physicians offer the type of care that *they* think is necessary, in consultation with their patients.

The proposal, which was strongly opposed by pro-life groups, passed by a margin of 2.2 million to 1.7 million votes. This victory was attributed to the efforts of ordinary citizens exercising their right to have a say in how they are governed. "I have a daughter and I really want to make sure that she has more rights than we do, not less rights,"[57] said Melissa Dobson, an Issue 1 supporter.

Other traditionally conservative states also saw pro-life efforts go down in defeat. After the *Dobbs* ruling, Kansas tried to add an amendment to its state constitution that would have denied the right to an abortion. Voters rejected the proposal 543,855 to 378,466.

A member of Kansans for Constitutional Freedom prepares for an election-results watch party. In August 2022 Kansas voters rejected a proposed amendment to the state constitution that would have denied the right to an abortion.

In Michigan, voters were asked to approve a measure, called the Right to Reproductive Freedom Initiative, which supported "the right to make and effectuate decisions about all matters relating to pregnancy, including but not limited to prenatal care, childbirth, postpartum care, contraception, sterilization, abortion care, miscarriage management, and infertility care."[58] In November 2022, the ballot measure passed with 56 percent of voters approving and 43 percent opposing. Although they came at it from different directions—Kansas putting up a pro-life measure and Michigan offering a pro-choice proposal—the result was the same: keeping abortion legal.

The story of abortion in the United States is still being written. As did *Roe* before it, the *Dobbs* decision unleashed powerful emotions on all sides of the abortion debate. That controversy continues.

SOURCE NOTES

Introduction: Life After the *Dobbs* Decision

1. Quoted in Tessa Weinberg, "Abortion Is Now Illegal in Missouri in Wake of U.S. Supreme Court Ruling," *Missouri Independent*, June 24, 2022. https://missouriindependent.com.
2. Quoted in Gloria Oladipo, "'One of Our Darkest Days': Outrage After Supreme Court Overturns Roe v Wade," *The Guardian*, June 24, 2022. www.theguardian.com.
3. Quoted in Chris Lisinski, "Massachusetts' Sweeping Reproductive Rights Bill Signed into Law," NBC Boston, July 29, 2022. www.nbcboston.com.
4. Quoted in Geoff Mulvihill, "One Year Later, the Supreme Court's Abortion Decision Is Both Scorned and Praised," Associated Press, June 24, 2023. https://apnews.com.
5. Quoted in Mulvihill, "One Year Later, the Supreme Court's Abortion Decision Is Both Scorned and Praised."
6. Quoted in Katia Riddle, "They Tried and Failed to Get an Abortion. Texas Family Grapples with What It'll Mean," NPR, June 22, 2023. www.npr.org.

Chapter One: The Road to *Dobbs*

7. US Supreme Court, *Dobbs v. Jackson Women's Health Organization*, majority opinion, June 24, 2022. www.supremecourt.gov/opinions/21pdf/19-1392_6j37.pdf.
8. US Supreme Court, *Dobbs v. Jackson Women's Health Organization*, majority opinion.
9. Joe Biden, "Remarks by President Biden on the Supreme Court Decision to Overturn *Roe v. Wade*," White House Briefing Room, June 24, 2022. www.whitehouse.gov.
10. Quoted in Reuters, "Reactions to the Supreme Court Overturning *Roe v. Wade*," June 26, 2022. www.reuters.com.
11. Quoted in Reuters, "Reactions to the Supreme Court Overturning *Roe v. Wade*."
12. Quoted in Reuters, "Reactions to the Supreme Court Overturning *Roe v. Wade*."
13. Quoted in Lauren Burke, "'Outrage and Action': Protesters Young and Old Gather Outside Supreme Court," *The Guardian*, June 24, 2022. www.theguardian.com.
14. Quoted in Sophia Barnes and NBC Washington Staff, "Protests Erupt at Supreme Court After Abortion Case Ruling," NBC4 Washington, June 25, 2022. www.nbcwashington.com.

15. Quoted in Editors of *Encyclopaedia Britannica*, "Roe v. Wade," Britannica, November 8, 2023. www.britannica.com.
16. Quoted in National Archives, "14th Amendment to the U.S. Constitution: Civil Rights (1868)." www.archives.gov.
17. Quoted in Editors of *Encyclopaedia Britannica*, "Roe v. Wade."
18. US Supreme Court, *Dobbs v. Jackson Women's Health Organization*, majority opinion.
19. US Supreme Court, *Dobbs v. Jackson Women's Health Organization*, dissenting opinion.

Chapter Two: Women at Risk

20. Quoted in Rebecca Boone, "Hypothetical Situations or Real-Life Medical Tragedies? A Judge Weighs an Idaho Abortion Lawsuit," Associated Press, December 14, 2023. https://apnews.com.
21. Quoted in Aria Bendix, "Woman Suing Texas over Abortion Ban Vomits on the Stand in Emotional Reaction During Dramatic Hearing," NBC News, July 19, 2023. www.nbcnews.com.
22. Quoted in Mary Tuma, "To Protect Her Twin Baby, Texas Woman Was Forced to Seek Abortion Care Out of State," Texas Public Radio, November 2, 2022. www.tpr.org.
23. Quoted in Kaylee Douglas, "Federal Complaint Filed Against Oklahoma Children's Hospital After Woman Denied Emergency Abortion," KFOR, September 12, 2023. https://kfor.com.
24. Quoted in Charlotte Alter, "She Wasn't Able to Get an Abortion. Now She's a Mom. Soon She'll Start 7th Grade," *Time*, August 14, 2023. https://time.com.
25. Quoted in Amy Schoenfeld Walker and Allison McCann, "Despite State Restrictions, Abortions in U.S. Increase as Overall Access Improves," *New York Times*, September 11, 2023. www.nytimes.com.
26. Lauren Leader, "The End of Roe Is Having a Chilling Effect on Pregnancy," *Politico*, September 13, 2023. www.politico.com.
27. Quoted in Leader, "The End of Roe Is Having a Chilling Effect on Pregnancy."

Chapter Three: Medical Professionals Under Fire

28. Quoted in Rachael Robertson, "A Year Later, Doctors Feel Impact of Dobbs Decision 'Every Single Day,'" MedPage Today, June 21, 2023. www.medpagetoday.com.
29. Quoted in Written testimony of Christina Francis, MD, for the Subcommittee on Oversight and Investigations of the Committee on Energy and Commerce hearing on "Roe Reversal: The Impacts of Taking Away the Constitutional Right to Abortion," July 16, 2022. https://aaplog.org.

30. Quoted in Stacy Weiner, "The Fallout of Dobbs on the Field of OB-GYN," AAMCNews, August 23, 2023. www.aamc.org.
31. Quoted in Selena Simmons-Duffin, "Doctors Who Want to Defy Abortion Laws Say It's Too Risky," *Shots* (blog), NPR, November 23, 2022. www.npr.org.
32. Quoted in Nadine El-Bawab, "Court Hears Arguments to Throw Out Tennessee Abortion Lawsuit, Block Ban in Part," ABC News, April 4, 2024. https://abcnews.go.com.
33. Quoted in Makenzie Huber, "Physicians Feel 'Trapped' by SD's Abortion Trigger Law. They're Hoping to Change It," *South Dakota Searchlight*, May 13, 2023. https://southdakotasearchlight.com.
34. Quoted in Kyle Pfannenstiel, "Idaho Is Losing OB-GYNs After Strict Abortion Ban. But Health Exceptions Unlikely This Year," *Idaho Capital Sun*, April 5, 2024. https://idahocapitalsun.com.
35. Quoted in Erin Snodgrass, "An Idaho Woman Who Documented Her 19-Day Miscarriage on TikTok Blames the State's Near-Total Abortion Ban for Her 'Horrific' Experience," Business Insider, December 30, 2022. www.businessinsider.com.
36. Quoted in Mary Kekatos, "Idaho Woman Shares 19-Day Miscarriage on TikTok, Says State's Abortion Laws Prevented Her from Getting Care," ABC News, January 21, 2023. https://abcnews.go.com.
37. Quoted in Sarah McCammon, "Doctors Rally to Defend Abortion Provider Caitlin Bernard After She Was Censured," *Weekend Edition Saturday*, NPR, June 3, 2023. www.npr.org.
38. Quoted in Peter Slevin, "One of the Last Abortion Doctors in Indiana," *New Yorker*, February 25, 2024. www.newyorker.com.
39. Quoted in Reena Diamante, "'We Have Already Reached Capacity': Abortion Clinics Overwhelmed by Out-of-State Travel," Spectrum News 1, August 31, 2022. https://spectrumnews1.com.
40. Quoted in Shefali Luthra, "'We Feel Kind of Powerless': The End of Roe Is Overwhelming Clinics in States That Protect Abortion," The 19th, July 15, 2022. https://19thnews.org.
41. Quoted in Luthra, "'We Feel Kind of Powerless.'"
42. Quoted in Sheryl Gay Stolberg, "Help for Risky Pregnancies Drops as Doctors Flee Abortion Limits," *New York Times*, September 7, 2023. www.nytimes.com.

Chapter Four: The Quest to End Abortion

43. Quoted in Jane Coaston, "After Ballot Losses, Where Does the Anti-Abortion Movement Go Next?," *New York Times*, August 21, 2023. www.nytimes.com.
44. Quoted in Holly Honderich, "She Helped Kill Roe v Wade—Now She Wants to End Abortion in America," BBC News, June 24, 2023. www.bbc.com.

45. Quoted in Nadine El-Bawab, "Abortion Pills Now Banned in Wyoming After Governor Signs Bill into Law," ABC News, March 18, 2023. https://abcnews.go.com.
46. Quoted in Elaine Godfrey, "The New Pro-Life Movement Has a Plan to End Abortion," *The Atlantic*, April 19, 2023. www.theatlantic.com.
47. Quoted in Pam Belluck and Adam Liptak, "Appeals Court Upholds Legality of Abortion Pill but with Significant Restrictions," *New York Times*, August 16, 2023. www.nytimes.com.
48. Quoted in Hanna Seariac, "The Activist Working to Reinvent America's Pro-Life Movement," *Deseret News* (Salt Lake City), November 6, 2023. www.deseret.com.
49. Quoted in Seariac, "The Activist Working to Reinvent America's Pro-Life Movement."
50. Quoted in National Archives, "14th Amendment to the U.S. Constitution."
51. Quoted in Amy Littlefield, "The Anti-Abortion Movement Gets a Dose of Post-*Roe* Reality," *The Nation*, June 28, 2023. www.thenation.com.
52. Quoted in Coaston, "After Ballot Losses, Where Does the Anti-Abortion Movement Go Next?"

Chapter Five: Efforts to Restore Abortion Rights

53. Quoted in Office of US Senator Patty Murray, "Murray, Schrier Reintroduce Legislation to Ensure Doctors Can Provide Legal Abortion Care, Protect Providers from Out of State Extremists," press release, April 26, 2023. www.murray.senate.gov.
54. Quoted in Office of Congresswoman Ayanna Pressley, "Pressley, Chu, Frankel, Escobar Lead 204 Colleagues to Introduce Women's Health Protection Act of 2023," press release, March 30, 2023. https://pressley.house.gov.
55. Quoted in Office of Governor Kathy Hochul, "On Eve of Dobbs Decision Anniversary, Governor Hochul Signs Legislation Strengthening Access to Reproductive Health Care," press release, June 23, 2023. www.governor.ny.gov.
56. Quoted in Lisa Rathke, "Vermont's Republican Governor Signs Abortion Pill Protections into Law," *PBS NewsHour*, May 10, 2023. www.pbs.org.
57. Quoted in Susan Tebben and Nick Evans, "Ohio Voters Pass Issue 1 Constitutional Amendment to Protect Abortion and Reproductive Rights," *Ohio Capital Journal*, November 7, 2023. https://ohiocapital journal.com.
58. Michigan Legislature, "State Constitution (Excerpt): Constitution of Michigan of 1963," Article 1, Section 28. www.legislature.mi.gov.

ORGANIZATIONS AND WEBSITES

Center for Reproductive Rights
https://reproductiverights.org
The Center for Reproductive Rights fights for laws and policies that protect and expand reproductive rights around the world. Its website contains resources and research on topics and issues that impact these rights.

Guttmacher Institute
www.guttmacher.org
The Guttmacher Institute is a research-based organization that advocates for greater sexual and reproductive health care around the world. Its website publishes fact-based data, articles, and reports on reproductive health policy issues.

National Right to Life Committee
www.nrlc.org
The NRLC works for the legal protection of every life, particularly the unborn, through education and political action. Its website contains news, legislative updates, and research material related to its mission.

Planned Parenthood
www.plannedparenthood.org
Planned Parenthood provides health care services for sexual and reproductive issues at clinics across the country. Its website contains clear, candid articles and resources on topics from abortion to birth control to gender identity.

Students for Life of America (SFLA)
https://studentsforlife.org
SFLA is an advocacy organization committed to abolishing abortion and supporting family-friendly policies in communities and the workplace. Its website contains articles and organizing material that advance its pro-life goals.

Susan B. Anthony (SBA) Pro-Life America
https://sbaprolife.org
SBA Pro-Life America is an antiabortion organization that seeks to elect pro-life leaders to national office. Its website tracks elections, politicians, voting records, and legal developments on matters related to its mission.

FOR FURTHER RESEARCH

Books

Merle Hoffman, *Choices: A Post-Roe Abortion Rights Manifesto*. New York: Skyhorse, 2023.

Carla Mooney, *Overturned: The Constitutional Right to Abortion*. San Diego: ReferencePoint, 2022.

Janet Morana, *Everything You Need to Know About Abortion: For Teens*. Gastonia, NC: TAN, 2022.

Lila Rose, *Fighting for Life: Becoming a Force for Change in a Wounded World*. Nashville: Thomas Nelson, 2021.

Meera Shah, *You're the Only One I've Told: The Stories Behind Abortion*. Chicago: Chicago Review, 2020.

Mary Ziegler, *Roe: The History of a National Obsession*. New Haven, CT: Yale University Press, 2023.

Internet Sources

Brennan Center for Justice, "Roe v. Wade and Supreme Court Abortion Cases," September 28, 2022. www.brennancenter.org.

Guttmacher Institute, "Interactive Map: US Abortion Policies and Access After Roe." https://states.guttmacher.org.

Caroline Kitchener, "An Abortion Ban Made Them Parents. This Is Life Two Years Later," *Washington Post*, August 1, 2023. www.washingtonpost.com.

Amy Littlefield, "'The Message They've Received Is That You Don't Deserve to Be Cared For': Life on the Abortion Borderland," *The Nation*, June 23, 2023. www.thenation.com.

Usha Ranji, Karen Diep, and Alina Salganicoff, "Key Facts on Abortion in the United States," KFF, November 21, 2023. www.kff.org.

WNYC Studios, "Part 1: The Viability Line," *More Perfect* (podcast), June 8, 2023. www.wnycstudios.org.

INDEX

Note: Boldface page numbers indicate illustrations.

abortion bans/restrictions, states leading in, 4–5
abortion restrictions
  efforts by young antiabortion crusaders, 37–40
  in history, 13–14
  on medication abortions, 40–42
  post-*Roe* trigger laws and, 4–6
  through fetal personhood laws, 43–45
abortion rights, efforts to protect/restore, 46–48
  ballot initiatives, 52–54
  lawsuits and, 51–52
  at state level, 48–51
  states at forefront of, 6, 19
abortion(s)
  ban on out-of-state travel for, 7
  cost of denial of, 22–24
  early attitudes/laws on, 12–14
  increase in, after *Dobbs* decision, 9
  most Americans support access to, 8–9
  number of women traveling out of state for, **20**
  public opinion on, **8**
  as routine care, 30
  young crusaders against, 37–40
Adkins, Jennifer, 19–20
Adkins, John, 20
affirmative defense requirements, 30–31
Alito, Samuel, 10–11, 17–18
Alliance for Hippocratic Medicine, 42
All In Together, 26
American Civil Liberties Union (ACLU), 51
antiabortion groups, view on *Dobbs* decision, 18

Arizona, 1864 law banning abortion in, 26
Arkansas, 4
  waiting period in, 47

Baker, Charlie, 6
ballot initiatives, 7, 52–54
Barrett, Amy Comey, 18
Bernard, Caitlin, 33–34, **34**
Biden, Joe, 11
Blackmun, Harry A., 16
Bowen-Marler, Emily, 53
Brandt, Ashley, 21–22
Breen, Peter, 7
Bresnan, Amy, 24
Bresnan, Steve, 24
Breyer, Stephen, 18
Broesder, Carmen, 32–33

California, 6
Center for Reproductive Rights, 51–52, 59
Cooper, Kylie, 35
counseling sessions, mandatory, 47–48

Dantas, Stella, 36
Davidson, Brittany, 31
DeSantis, Ron, 39
DeWine, Mike, 52
Dobbs v. Jackson Women's Health Organization (2022)
  abortion restriction laws triggered by, 4–6
  as energizing pro-choice movement, 46
  public reaction to, 6–7
Dobson, Melissa, 53
doctors
  forced to relocate from abortion-restrictive states, 35
  risk of prosecution of, 29–32

Echelon Insights, 26

fetal personhood, 43, 44
   state laws requiring women to be
      told of, 48
Florida, 39
Food and Drug Administration, US
   (FDA), 40, 42
Fourteenth Amendment, 16–17
   move for fetal personhood
      recognized under, 44
Francis, Christina, 29
Freedom to Travel for Health Care Act
   (proposed), 48

Gordon, Mark, 41
Gorsuch, Neil, 18
Graham, Lindsay, 40
Guttmacher Institute, 9, 59
   on deaths from illegal abortions, 14
   on number of women traveling out of
      state for abortions, 21
   on states banning/restricting
      abortion, 24–25

Hawkins, Kristan, 37–40, **38**, 45
Hobbs, Katie, 26
Hochul, Kathy, 50

I Am Roe (McCorvey), 13
Idaho, 5
   challenge to abortion law in, 52
incest exceptions, 14, 26, 40, 52
   antiabortion groups oppose, 42–43

James, Letitia, 51
Johnson, Alexis McGill, 26–27

Kagan, Elena, 18
Kavanaugh, Brett, 18
Kugler, Sara, 12

Let Doctors Provide Reproductive
   Health Care Act (proposed), 46–47
Live Action (anti-abortion group), 42,
   43

Mace, Nancy, 43
Massachusetts, 6

McConnell, Mitch, 11
McCorvey, Norma, 13, 14–15, **15**
McHugh, Katie, 30
medication abortion(s), 40
   efforts to ban, 41–42
   efforts to protect, 49–50
Michigan, pro-choice ballot initiative
   in, 54
mifepristone, 40–41, **41**, 42, **50**,
   50–51
Minnesota, 6
misoprostol, 33, 40, 41, 50
Mississippi, 4
Missouri
   ballot measure for abortion rights in,
      53
   trigger law in, 4–5
   waiting period in, 47
Missourians for Constitutional Freedom
   (MCF), 53

National Right to Life Committee, 59
Nevada, 6
New Mexico, 25, **25**
NewsHour/NPR/Marist poll, 18
New York
   as first state allowing abortion, 14
   protection for medication abortion in,
      49–51
New York Times (newspaper), 25
North Carolina, number of consent
   forms required in, 31

Ohio, 28, 33
   ballot initiative to protect abortion
      rights in, 7, 52–53
opinion polls. *See* surveys

Pelosi, Nancy, 11
Pence, Mike, 11, 40
Peters, Kelly, 36
Planned Parenthood, 42, 59
   percentage of services related to
      abortion, 39
Planned Parenthood of Southeastern
   Pennsylvania v. Casey (1992), 16
polls. *See* surveys

pregnancy
  women avoiding due to concerns
    about emergency medical care, 26
  women's unsafe attempts to end, 14
Pressley, Ayanna, 48
Pritzker, J.B., 49
privacy, 51
  Fourteenth Amendment and, 16–17
pro-choice movement, **47**
  Dobbs decision as energizing, 46

quickening, 13

rape exceptions, 14, 26, 40, 52
  antiabortion groups oppose, 42–43
Right to Reproductive Freedom
  Initiative (MI), 54
Roberts, John, 18
Roe v. Wade (1973), 4, 10
  plaintiff in, 13, 14–15, **15**
  Supreme Court ruling on, 15–17
  woman behind, 13, 14–15, **15**
Rokita, Todd, 33
Rose, Lila, 43–45, **44**, 45
Rust, Lynn, 6

Schipper, Erica, 31–32
Schmitt, Eric, 4–5
Schrier, Kim, 47
Schumer, Chuck, 6
Scott, Phil, 51
Smith, Elisabeth, 39
Sotomayor, Sonia, 18
South Carolina, 5, 43
South Carolina Prenatal Equal
  Protection Act (2023), 43
South Dakota, 4
Statton, Jaci, 22–23
Students for Life of America (SFLA),
  37, 59
Supreme Court, **5**
  ruling *in Dobbs*, 10–11

ruling *in Roe*, 15–17
surveys
  on federal law granting right to
    abortion, 45
  on legality of abortion, **8**, 9
  of ob-gyn doctors feeling
    constrained in providing care, 30
  on protecting abortion freedoms,
    18
  on women avoiding pregnancy due
    to concerns about emergency
    medical care, 26
Susan B. Anthony (SBA) Pro-Life
  America, 59

Texas, 21
  challenge to abortion law in, 49,
    51–52
Think Big America (social welfare
  organization), 49
Thomas, Clarence, 18
travel, out-of-state for abortion, 19–21,
  33
  number of women forced into, **20**
  proposed law protecting right of, 48
trigger laws, 4
Truehart, Amber, 35

unborn, legal rights for, 45
"undue burden" test, 16

Vermont, 6

Wade, Henry, 15
waiting periods, mandated, 16
Weinerman, Rachel, 28
Whitlock, Brian, 32
Women's Health Protection Act
  (proposed, 2023), 47
Wyoming, 5

Zurawski, Amanda, 49

PICTURE CREDITS

Cover: behzad moloud/Shutterstock (left);
Vic Hinterlang/Shutterstock (right)

5: AC NewsPhoto/Alamy Stock Photo
8: Maury Aaseng
12: Associated Press
15: Ron Sachs -CNP/picture alliance/Consolidated News Photos/Newscom
20: Maury Aaseng
23: Yuri Arcurs/Alamy Stock Photo
25: Victor Maschek/Shutterstock
29: Rocketclips, Inc./Shutterstock
34: Sue Dorfman/ZUMAPRESS/Newscom
36: Associated Press
38: Associated Press
41: Associated Press
44: Ron Sachs/picture alliance / Consolidated News Photos/Newscom
47: Andreas Stroh/Alamy Stock Photo
50: Brigette Supernova/Alamy Stock Photo
54: Tammy Ljungblad/TNS/Newscom

ABOUT THE AUTHOR

Robert Lerose has been a writer since 1994. His magazine articles have appeared in *Highlights*, *Boys' Life*, and *Boys' Quest*. He is the author of four nonfiction books for young people. In 2004 he won the Great American Think-Off, a philosophy competition open to people of all ages. He lives on Long Island, New York.